# Summertime Idioms

Lisa Velez-Batista

Illustrated By: Ivan Earl-Aguilar

Colored By: Frances Espanol

ISBN: Softcover 978-1-5035-8323-8
Hardcover 978-1-9845-2594-9
EBook 978-1-5035-8322-1



Print information available on the last page.

Rev. date: 07/23/2015

To order additional copies of this book, contact:
Xlibris
1-888-795-4274
www.Xlibris.com
Orders@Xlibris.com

# Summertime Idioms

Lisa Velez-Batista
Illustrated By: Ivan Earl-Aguilar
Colored By: Frances Espanol

When **the dog days of summer** are very hot,

a sprinkler on the block is the coolest spot.

If you can earn money while having fun,

you have found your **place in the sun**.

LEMONADE
25 ¢

**A drop in the ocean** isn't much you see.

It's the smallest unit of the mighty sea.

wish we could take a trip
n a cruise ship one day.
You can have the money
in my piggy bank.
Thanks but that’s just a
drop in the ocean. We would
need much more than that.

If you want to **beat the heat**,

a nautical retreat might be neat.

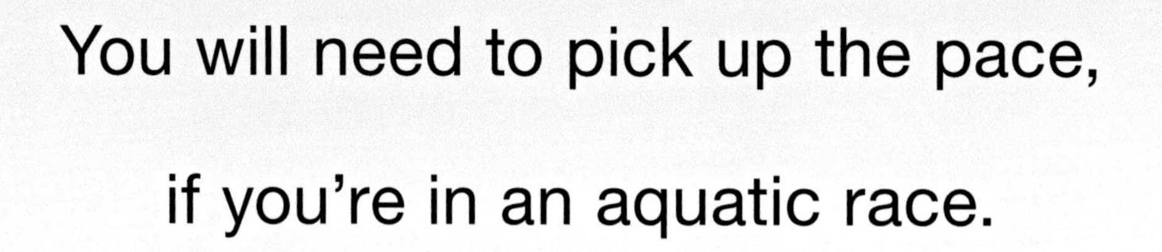

You will need to pick up the pace,

if you’re in an aquatic race.

**The heat is on** if you want to win.

No one can help you, not even your kin.

Upon your face will be a grin,

as you accept the prize you'll win.

**In a flash,** you'll **make a splash.**

It may not be good for one who jogs,

when **it's raining cats and dogs**.

If your plans are a wreck,

you will need **a rain check.**

I won't be able to go running with you today but maybe we can go tomorrow.

After all the work is done,

it is time to have some fun.

Do not think about failing,

from here on it’s **smooth sailing.**

You are doing it Andrew!
Wait for me Chris!

If you get **hot under the collar**,

don't scream, yell or holler.

Everything will turn out fine.

There will be **a ray of sunshine.**

# GLOSSARY

**A drop in the ocean:** a very small amount compared to what is needed

**A place in the sun:** a good or lucky position

**A rain check:** something you say when you cannot accept someone's invitation to do something but you would like to do it another time

**A ray of sunshine:** someone or something that makes you feel happy

**Beat the heat:** to escape the heat of summer

**Dog days of summer:** the hottest and muggiest days of summer (July through August)

**Hot under the collar:** to be very angry

**In a flash:** right away, immediately

**It's raining cats and dogs:** it's raining heavily

**Make a splash:** to get a lot of public attention

**Smooth sailing:** easy progress

**The heat is on:** a time of great activity and/or pressure has begun

## About the Author

**Lisa Velez-Batista** began her career as a Speech and Language Therapist in Brooklyn, NY where she was born and raised. It has been her dream to write a book that would enable children to enhance their language skills. Her seasonal books were written to help children improve their knowledge of figurative language; however, they can also be used to help improve phonemic awareness and category skills. Worksheets for all of her books are available at lisavelez-batista.com.

Printed in the United States
By Bookmasters